GRASS-WIDOWS
Sisyrinchium douglasii
Pine Creek Auto Tour Route
Turnbull National Wildlife Refuge
Spokane County, Washington
April 27, 1996

ARROWLEAF BALSAMROOT *Balsamorhiza sagittata*
BROADLEAF LUPINE *Lupinus latifolius* var. *thompsonianus*
BARESTEM DESERT PARSLEY *Lomatium nudicale*

Dallas Mountain Road, Columbia Hills
Klickitat County, Washington
April 22, 1997

BROADLEAF LUPINE *Lupinus latifolius*
WHITE BOG ORCHID *Habenaria dilatata* var. *dilatata*

Crystal Springs in Kelsey Valley, Umpqua National Forest
Cascade Range, Oregon
July 2, 1986

BROADLEAF LUPINE *Lupinus latifolius*
MAGENTA PAINTBRUSH *Castilleja parviflora* var. *oreopola*

Tipsoo Lake and Mount Rainier
Mount Rainier National Park, Cascade Range, Washington
August 6, 1996

Opposite: BROWN'S PEONY *Paeonia brownii*
Forest Road 453, Goose Creek Canyon
Payette National Forest, Adams County, Idaho
May 16, 1997

Wildflowers
OF THE PACIFIC NORTHWEST

Photography by
LARRY ULRICH

Interpretive text by Susan Lamb

COMPANION PRESS
SANTA BARBARA, CALIFORNIA

SPREADING PHLOX *Phlox diffusa*
Slate Peak, Forest Road 600
Mount Baker-Snoqualamie National Forest
North Cascade Range, Washington
August 3, 1997

© 1999 Companion Press
All photographs © Larry Ulrich
Text essay © 1999 Susan Lamb

All Rights Reserved
Companion Press
464 Terrace Road
Santa Barbara, California 93109

Jane Freeburg, Publisher/Editor
Designed by Lucy Brown
Printed and bound in Hong Kong
through Bolton Associates, San Rafael, California
ISBN 0-944197-57-4 (paperback)
ISBN 0-944197-58-2 (clothbound)

99 00 01 02 03   5 4 3 2 1

Contents

PREFACE
by Donna B. Ulrich   9

NORTHWEST WILD FLORA
by Susan Lamb   13

PHOTOGRAPHIC PORTFOLIO   32
104 images by Larry Ulrich

PHOTOGRAPHER'S NOTES   136

SUBALPINE BUTTERCUP
Ranunculus eschscholtzii

Headwaters Little Blitzen River
Steens Mountain, Andrews Resource Area
Bureau of Land Management
Harney County, Oregon
August 4, 1997

OLYMPIC MOUNTAIN PAINTBRUSH *Castilleja parviflora* var. *olympica*
BROADLEAF LUPINE *Lupinus latifolius*
AMERICAN BISTORT *Polygonum bistortoides*

Hurricane Ridge near Eagle Point
Olympic National Park
Olympic Mountains, Washington
August 1, 1997

SCARLET GILIA
Gilia aggregata
WHITE SWERTIA
Swertia montana
Highway 55
Little Goose Creek Valley
Payette National Forest, Idaho
June 29, 1997

Preface

Our introduction to botany of the Pacific Northwest began in the Olympic Mountains of Washington, where we were spending the summer photographing, hiking and learning about the native plants of the region. Gray Wolf was the "pass *du jour*" that crisp July morning and we were not looking forward to the 3,500-foot climb. We had already been humbled by lesser passes that summer, but we knew this trail would pass through open meadows and hanging gardens and that was why we had chosen this path.

We dropped our packs to get a drink of water before the trail started climbing and as we gazed up at the switchbacks fading into the mist, a line of hikers appeared from the direction we had come. As they passed we couldn't help but notice the new, straight-from-R.E.I. packs they were carrying. There was no dirt, no bulging zippers, nothing but Sierra Club cups hung from their packs. Absent also was the proud flag of the Pacific Northwest hiker—wet socks dangling from sleeping bag straps, "drying." We looked down at our own worn and overstuffed packs with horror! Larry's pack was full of camera gear and weighed more than sixty pounds, mine was over forty pounds. We had to carry those things up that trail.

After the line of cheerful faces had passed we shouldered our packs to step out onto the trail, but paused to let two stragglers go by. Funny, they didn't look like they were with the Happy Hikers. Two grizzled men of about forty-something were carrying dirty packs with bulging zippers and the soggy flag of the Pacific Northwest hiker. They paused, looking relieved to be dismissed from the parade, and the big, bearded guy said "We're not with them," as if to answer our unspoken question. "I'm Bill" the other one said with a smile, "and this is Dick. He's trying to teach me about the plants. Are you going our way?"

Soon we were trudging up the windy trail, getting to know each other with each step. We found that our new friends were old college buddies sharing a week-long hike together. When we found that Dick was an amateur botanist Larry started asking questions.

"Is this a lupine?" Larry asked Dick.

"*Lupinus latifolius*," Dick answered, using the Latin name.

A few switchbacks later, we spotted another interesting species and ventured a guess. "Is that a valerian?"

"Sitka valerian, *Valeriana sitchensis*," Dick answered without hesitation.

Eventually we came to one of the hanging gardens we were hoping to see and stopped for photographs and a snack. Larry scanned for unusual flowers, saw something new and challenged Dick once again. "What is this one with the tiny flowers?"

"Hmm, a willow herb of sorts," said Dick. "Let's look it up and key it out." With that, Dick reached into his pack and brought out a worn-out plastic bag with a University of Washington logo on it, and from it he removed a copy of Hitchcock's *Flora of the Pacific Northwest*. Larry was surprised and impressed that Dick had carried this book with him, because the volume weighed almost four pounds dry and it wasn't. Suddenly we realized that Dick was not just a weekend walker, he was a serious student of botany, a wealth of knowledge with a very cool book. Thus began our initiation into the flowering plants of the Pacific Northwest. The hike up Gray Wolf Pass took most of the day, but each step brought new botanical wonders, more questions and as many answers.

That evening we camped together and swapped stories of lofty peaks and pristine streams. Tired feet were forgotten and memories of quiet paths and powerful sunsets ushered in the night. We talked of tree-lined lakes and meadows brimming with wildflowers. Bill described hikes he'd done outside his native Portland and Dick shared his love of Washington. We traveled, through their stories, across the Pacific Northwest, from the Pasayten Wilderness on the Canadian border south to the Rogue River of Oregon, to the wind-blown beaches of Bandon to the Palouse land of eastern Washington. Although Larry and I live on the "botanical edge" of the Pacific Northwest, we had never fully understood or studied the diversity hidden within the

RED MOUNTAIN HEATHER
Phyllodoce empetriformis
~and Mount Rainier

Skyline Trail, Paradise Park
Mount Rainier National Park
Cascade Range, Washington
August 6, 1996

common borders of Oregon, Washington and parts of Idaho. Now we had clues, little snippets of information, and as we snuggled in our sleeping bags that fine July evening, Larry told me that he would love to photograph a book on the wildflowers of the Pacific Northwest someday.

"Someday" turned out to be twenty years later. Larry now carries his own dog-eared, duct-taped copy of Hitchcock into the wilderness. He's a very good amateur botanist and together we've logged enough miles in the three northwestern states to have stories of our own and photographs to prove it. We have followed every lead we get—for example, a Bureau of Land Management botanist told us to go to Camas County in Idaho to look for fields of common Camas. A Nature Conservancy docent led us to where giant helleborine grows, only to find the beautiful orchid surrounded by an impenetrable fortress of poison ivy. We didn't get that shot, nor did we get a rash. My brother and sister-in-law told us of their favorite flower fields in Idaho—we were ready to go when the road to Trinity Lakes was cleared of snow that summer and found it to be everything they promised.

Our research helped us find where to look for many of the species, but some we simply stumbled upon. While driving through Tumwater Canyon in the Washington Cascades, I spotted a salmon-colored flower, which turned out to be a Tweedy's lewisia, a showy species we'd been looking for. We found several outcroppings full of this endangered plant and made some fine photographs of it.

This volume, our third foray into the field of wildflower books (*Wildflowers of California* and *Wildflowers of the Plateau and Canyon Country* are the other two) is not intended to be a field guide but a visual interpretation of the diversity, abundance and beauty of the Pacific Northwest's native flora. Still, we encourage the reader to take this book into the field for inspiration and fun—and unlike Hitchcock's opus, it weighs far less than four pounds! We thank the many people who shared their knowledge of wildflowers with us, especially those two friendly hikers on Gray Wolf Pass. We haven't hiked with Dick in many years and Bill has had bypass surgery, but we still swap memories with them. Two decades ago, we had two strangers invite us to explore the Pacific Northwest, and now it is our turn. Are you going our way?

Donna Bacon Ulrich

Cow parsnip *Heracleum lanatum*

Lemolo Falls, North Umpqua River
Umpqua National Forest, Cascade Range, Oregon
July 2, 1986

Northwest Wild Flora

My soul can find no staircase to Heaven unless it be through Earth's loveliness.
—Michelangelo

There is nothing stingy or meager about the rainforest of the Pacific Northwest. All of life's essentials, especially water and sunlight, are in great abundance here. Life exults in a seamless tangle of roots and twining stems, in an orgy of burgeoning growth. Plants drape branches, festoon boulders, and sprout from stumps under the toes of shiny, chartreuse tree frogs. Foliate lichens unfurl on the gray bark of spruce trees, glistening slugs ooze along footpaths thick with fallen needles, caterpillars tightrope across twigs hung with opalescent raindrops backlit by morning sun…even the rain sifting down seems to be alive as we listen to it breathe and sigh and hush, pause and sigh and then sift down again.

Many days here are so completely sodden that we can recall without effort how it felt to be bits of protoplasm floating in the primordial soup. The coast of the Pacific Northwest receives more precipitation than anywhere else on our continent north of Guatemala. Massive trees up to three hundred feet tall thrive here in the only temperate rainforest in the northern hemisphere. Some of them, western red cedars for instance, may be as old as a thousand years.

Giant fawn-lily
Erythronium oregonum

Forest Road 25
Hamma Hamma River Canyon
Olympic National Forest
Olympic Mountains
Washington
April 6, 1996

DWARF MONKEYFLOWER
Mimulus nanus
Loop Road, Craters of the Moon
National Monument
Butte County, Idaho
June 4, 1996

Yet often in this imposing and magnificent forest, what most intrigues us is the luminous little face of a wood nymph, or the occasional fairy lantern nodding in the rain. It may seem frivolous to focus on wildflowers when the world has so many problems. Yet it is worth remembering that without flowering plants, we humans would simply cease to exist. I recall hiking one morning with a vigorous old fellow named Jerry, a retired businessman from Manhattan who had been a mover and shaker his whole life. When I pointed out a patch of humble forget-me-nots and solemnly announced *Myosotis sylvatica*, Jerry just had to laugh. "Oh, that's so esoteric!" he hooted. "What about the real world?" He bent to sniff the little flowers and then all at once straightened up, gazing into the distance in pursuit of his train of thought. Smiling wistfully, he murmured, "This is the real world, isn't it?"

Like many others of my generation, I grew up somewhat alienated from an increasingly urban society. It seemed that something important was being ignored, but I couldn't figure out what it might be. I became discouraged for no apparent reason and tottered into adolescence a pale and gloomy waif. Fortunately, an opportunity for work took my family and me to a tiny settlement in the rainforest of the Pacific Northwest. I fell in with some rough children there who prowled the woods in search of fairy slippers, foraging on salmon berries and wild honey, and discovered within myself an affinity for plants in general and an unutterable tenderness for flowers. In a few short months I regained my health, and it didn't surprise me a bit when later I learned that chlorophyll—the lifeblood of plants—is structured very like human hemoglobin except that it is centered on an atom of magnesium instead of iron. To this day, my great love as a naturalist is the infinite variety and loveliness of the plant kingdom. Wildflowers will always remind me of how good it is simply to be alive.

Coast fawn lily
Erythronium revolutum
Saddle Mountain State Park
Coast Range
Clatsop County, Oregon
May 3, 1996

Life is wet. The ocean, the original wetness and once the cradle of life, still quenches the thirst of all living things, on land even to the mountaintops.

—Stewart T. Schultz, *The Northwest Coast*

    Wildflowers of the Pacific Northwest are clearly children of the ocean. Weather records tell us that the average rainy season lasts about six months here, although many would argue that it never ends. The rains usually begin in November, as water evaporating from the warm Japanese Current forms clouds over the Pacific. Moving eastward over Washington and Oregon, these sodden air masses drench the coast with anywhere from forty-five inches of rain to twice that much, reviving lush meadows, banks of ferns, berry bushes, and marshes. As they encounter higher elevations of even a few hundred feet, the clouds release more and more precipitation, inundating the Olympic Peninsula's Hoh River Valley with an amazing twelve feet of rain and the Olympic Mountains with as much as two hundred inches—more than sixteen feet—of rain and snow. Sequim—at the eastern base of the Olympics—receives a mere seventeen inches, but Seattle and the rest of the Puget Trough get about forty. Enough snow falls on the Cascades themselves to sustain glaciers of packed snow and ice (there are twenty-six glaciers on Mount Rainier alone). Oregon's rainfall pattern is very similar to that of Washington.

    In eastern Washington and Oregon, the "rainshadow" of the Cascades creates a Great Basin ecosystem of buckwheats and locoweeds on high interior steppes that receive less than twenty inches of precipitation a year. Despite forests of thunderheads, not much rain actually hits the ground there during the summer. The region's huge wheat fields, extensive orchards, and thriving vineyards must be irrigated by the canals and streams of the Columbia Basin. Where untouched by plows and pumps, drought-tolerant purple sage and barestem desert parsley brighten the fertile soil of this interior; golden spiderflower and nakedstem sunray gild its badlands and sand dunes. Where mountains punch up through these eastern reaches, they wring moisture out of the clouds to support forests and flowers of a high desert character.

However, ninety percent of the Pacific Northwest's infamous rain and snow falls from November to April, when few plants are blooming. Plants and soil retain some of this moisture but as the days lengthen into summer, vernal pools shrink and waterfalls dwindle to a few sparkles on baking basalt cliffs. Summer "fog-drip" increases the total precipitation along the coast by as much as ten or twenty percent, and fogs from the ocean do reach some distance inland to condense on leaves, but patterns of precipitation do not entirely explain the abundance of wildflowers in the Pacific Northwest.

> *Be praised, my Lord, for all your creatures,*
> *and first for brother sun,*
> *who makes the day bright and luminous.*
> *And he is beautiful and radiant*
> *with great splendor....*
> —SAINT FRANCIS OF ASSISI, *The Canticle of the Sun*

Flowers, in fact, are exuberant proof of the abundance of summer sunlight in northern latitudes. Although we humans often complain that we never see the sun here, plants perceive it readily enough. The number of daylight hours increases rapidly in the Pacific Northwest after the spring equinox in March. By the summer solstice (June 20 or 21), there are fifteen hours of sunlight at latitude 40°, while midsummer days at the 50° parallel are over sixteen hours long. Plants flourish in response to these long days because they "eat" sunlight, absorbing it in their chlorophyll. They use this solar energy to synthesize carbohydrates from carbon dioxide and water, then store the carbohydrates as tissue. This means, basically, that the more sunlight they get, the more plants can grow.

NAKEDSTEM SUNRAY
Enceliopsis nudicaulis
Bruneau Dunes State Park
Owyhee County, Idaho
May 13, 1996

Sunlight also triggers the blooming of many flowers. Most flowers must exchange pollen with others of their kind in order to develop seeds, and the majority of them depend upon insects, birds, or bats to carry out this transfer. Together with a sort of inborn "biological clock," sunlight signals plants to begin flowering when the days are long enough for the appropriate bugs or birds to be in the neighborhood. To time their blossoming, plants measure the number of hours of sunlight in a day with a pigment in their tissues called phytochrome. They bloom only after their phytochrome absorbs the right amount of red or near-red light from the sun.

Many spring flowers are perennials that bloom year after year. Most develop from bulbs, corms, or rosettes of overwintering leaves, which are all forms of stored nourishment that can give them a head start on the season. Spring flowers tend to be small, few in number, and subtle like valerian, kittentails, and Dutchman's breeches. They open on the coast with the emerging insects and returning birds of April. A few weeks later, they begin to bloom on foothills and in the interior. Several weeks after that, they appear on the highest mountains. Violets, the quintessential symbols of spring, follow this pattern: stream violets *(Viola glabella)* bloom on the coast around April Fool's Day, some weeks before early blue violets *(Viola adunca)* appear far upstream in the canyons of Idaho and long before marsh violets *(Viola palustris)* blossom on Mount Rainier in June.

Flowering plants require minimums and maximums of warmth as well as light. It can be very cold in dry or high-elevation areas; plants wait until the soil is warm enough before they bloom. Delicate blossoms of shooting star and spring beauty emerge shyly for only a brief spell between the freezing temperatures of spring and autumn in the high Olympics, the Cascades, and the Sawtooth Mountains of Idaho.

The Navajo have a strong feeling for plants, which they treat with the greatest respect. The symbol for life and productivity, for peace and prosperity, is pollen. Pollen symbolizes light.
—Stephen Jett, *Navajo Wildlands*

Sooner or later, summer arrives with great sweeps of bright and colorful wildflowers, some of which exude clouds of fragrance in order to attract passing pollinators. Various kinds of sunflowers are especially common in summer, their characteristic daisy-shaped heads appealing to lots of different flies, bees, butterflies, and beetles. Although many summer flowers attract human attention because they are yellow or orange, they lure insects to their pollen with ultraviolet lines and dots that are invisible to us.

Pollen is made up of nutritious proteins and flavored with sugars. Flowers originally evolved appetizing pollen to attract hungry beetles, who were dusted with some of it as they ate and inadvertently carried it to the next flower. Lots of insects and other animals still visit flowers mainly to eat pollen; primitive moths fork it out of wide-open marsh marigolds with a sort of claw and stuff it into their gnashing mandibles. Flowers can be very choosy: rhododendrons release their pollen only to certain bees, who know how to grab the flowers' pollen-producing anthers and buzz their flight muscles to shake it out.

Most flowers now produce nectar as an additional attraction, using color and scent to advertise when it is available. Birds are not sensitive to fragrance, but certain bees and butterflies collect what is called the "odor substance" itself, in order to perfume themselves for courtship. Some flowers offer nectar only at certain times; subalpine daisies provide morning nectar to flies, for example. Certain shapes restrict nectar to moths and butterflies that have a long proboscis which they keep curled up like a paper party tooter and unfurl to probe flowers. Things don't always work out the way they are supposed to, though: the long spur petals of columbines are designed for hummingbird tongues but bees sometimes bite through to "steal" nectar pooled there.

BIGLEAF LUPINE
Lupinus polyphyllus var. *polyphyllus*

RED COLUMBINE
Aquilegia formosa

Forest Road 65
Panther Creek Canyon
Gifford Pinchot National Forest
Cascade Range, Washington
June 7, 1996

In addition to pollen, scent, and high-energy nectar, flowers have other ways to attract specific pollinators. Orchids and irises, for instance, produce oils that female bees mop up with their brushy forelegs and deposit with their eggs for emerging larvae to eat. Some flowers that close up in the evenings, like linearleaf daisies, protect the bugs within their petals from frost and wind to ensure that they will be alive (and caked with pollen) in the morning. Skunk cabbage not only shelters flies in its enfolding spathe, but generates a measurable warmth to keep them cozy and active all night.

Landscape is the firstborn of Creation.
—JOHN O'DONAGHUE, *Anam Cara*

The ancients saw the world as consisting of four essences: earth, air, water, and fire. From a flowering plant's point of view, this is still a useful way to perceive things. Each flower's habitat—its natural home—has the right soil as well as adequate moisture, tolerable temperatures, and favorable exposure to sun and wind. The Pacific Northwest encompasses a great many different habitats including moist seacoasts, cool mountains, and arid plains. It has forested peninsulas embraced by water, prairies swept by wind, deserts wrapped in silence, cool and lofty peaks. Within each of these habitats, local factors such as sand dunes or bedrock create smaller ecological niches. This is true especially along the Columbia River Gorge, where myriad specially-adapted wildflowers—midget phlox, popcorn flower, and upland larkspur—bloom in niches defined by black basalt bluffs and ravines.

Oregon offers much more than Oregon grape, its state flower, in large part because of its varied soils. Washington, too, has more than rhododendrons glowing incandescent in spruce groves. Because it has so many habitats with so many different soils, the Pacific Northwest is an amazingly varied floral province.

Nature is a part of our humanity, and without some awareness and experience of that divine mystery, man ceases to be man.
—Henry Beston, *The Outermost House*

For some time now, science educators have been pushing the idea of "biodiversity." They keep trying to tell us how important biodiversity is to the wellbeing of ourselves and the planet. However, a recent series of focus groups set up by the research team Belden and Russonello show that few of us—from any background or level of education—respond to the word or appreciate the idea behind it. To most people, "biodiversity" sounds like a bunch of loose, interchangeable parts.

Flowers are like faces: they are the part of a plant that speaks to us. They transform the sterile term "biodiversity" into sweet images that persuade us to care more about biodiversity than the word itself possibly could. One of the first things each flower tells us is who its partners are. Every flower's color, scent, and shape are precisely designed to attract the right bugs or birds to carry its pollen to other flowers of its kind. Should a species of flower be lost forever, its pollinating partners may be doomed as well.

Think of just one kind of flower and ask yourself, "What if there were suddenly no more of these? Would it really matter so much?" If evening primroses suddenly disappeared, it would matter a great deal indeed to the moths who depend upon their nectar and pollen, and whose caterpillars use the buds as nurseries. It would matter to the goldfinches that eat some of the six thousand or so seeds produced by each plant. And what would happen to the many other creatures who feed and take cover among the plant's early rosettes and mature stalks? Evening primroses also aid other flowering plants, sheltering their seedlings and holding bare soil in place by colonizing disturbed areas. Would it matter much to human beings if evening primroses became extinct? It might matter to some of us. Evening primrose oil contains gamma-linolenic acid, an essential fatty acid used to treat everything from arthritis to eczema, migraines to schizophrenia, obesity to asthma, clotting disorders, and even weak fingernails. Now consider this: evening primroses are just one of a hundred or so genera that are pictured in this book.

> *We are dust and to dust we shall return.*
> *In the end we're*
> *neither air, nor fire, nor water,*
> *just*
> *dirt,*
> *neither more nor less, just dirt,*
> *and maybe*
> *some yellow flowers.*
> —PABLO NERUDA, *Ode to Some Yellow Flowers*

The plant kingdom is a glorious tangle of chaos and intent, a marvel that we are incapable of creating ourselves. Although it is certainly possible to classify wildflowers, investigate the chemical reactions of their life processes, and dissect them down to their constituent atoms, we cannot entirely explain them. Scientists refer to "emergent properties," which are the qualities that vanish when living things are picked apart down to the level of their molecules. At some point in such studies, researchers suddenly realize that they are examining lifeless parts and must reverse direction in their search to understand how living things function. Before the advent of modern science, philosophers had a name for the animating force that quickens earth, air, water, and the sun's fire into life; they called it the quintessence. Whatever we call it—emergent property or quintessence or life force or whatever—it is something that we cannot duplicate. No amount of computer programming or laboratory simulation can approach it.

We live with such material abundance and are surrounded by so much virtual reality that it is all too easy to disregard the natural world today. That is, until we encounter a wildflower. Flowering plants are symbols of life itself, epiphanies of love and beauty. They sustain other forms of life from molds to mosquitoes, sparrows to ground squirrels, and even the coyotes who eat berries in the fall. Flowers speak to us of biodiversity in terms we can understand: "Look how many different shapes and scents and colors we have! Think of our countless partnerships with the insects, birds, and mammals who may eat us, yes, but who transfer our pollen and transport our seeds so that we will endure for countless generations." Flowers caution us to be gentle with living things, for once we destroy life we cannot restore it. We know that there are many practical reasons to conserve biodiversity, but flowers are also vivid reminders that, as Thomas Berry has written, "To wantonly destroy a living species is to silence forever a divine voice."

> *All rootedness is learning to call things by the right name.*
> —CONFUCIUS

For many people, it is enough just to experience wildflowers without analyzing them. But an international study—made in 1998 by the World Conservation Union (IUCN) in conjunction with the Smithsonian Institution—indicates that nearly one of every three plants in the United States is threatened with extinction, having fewer than ten thousand individuals worldwide or fewer than one hundred locations in which it is found. Once we realize how casually flowers are disregarded these days, it can seem more important to learn at least something about them.

There are certainly many ways to get to know wildflowers. An obvious place to start is to learn their names. Both common and scientific names are helpful. A fairy slipper, for instance, looks like a tiny, pink slipper. But where might it be found? In the *Audubon Society Field Guide to North American Wildflowers*, Richard Spellenberg uses its scientific name, *Calypso bulbosa*, as a clue:

> Named for the sea nymph Calypso of Homer's Odyssey, who detained the willing Odysseus on his return from Troy; like Calypso, the plant is beautiful and prefers secluded haunts.

BACH'S DOWNINGIA
Downingia bacigalupii

LEAST NAVARRETIA
Navarretia minima

TANSY-LEAF EVENING-PRIMROSE
Camissonia tanacetifolia

Vernal pools along Silver Creek
Sage Hen Valley
Highway 20 near Riley
Harney County, Oregon
June 30, 1997

The common names of flowers can tell us lots of things. Manroot has a branching, human-like tuber, for instance. Skunk cabbage stinks to attract flies; evening primroses wait until twilight to open and scent the air sweetly for moths. However, a flower can have many common names. Two hikers could quibble forever over whether what they saw back there was a pussy ear or a mariposa lily, only to check a field guide and discover they are both talking about *Calochortus tolmie*.

Taxonomy is the scientific system of naming plants in Latin, a language that is considered universal because no one actually speaks it any more, and consistent because it is no longer evolving. Taxonomy may seem complicated, but it does make sense. First, botanists sort flowers into families: groups of flowering plants that share certain characteristics. Any flower in *Fabaceae*, the pea family, will have certain features whether it is a beach pea from San Juan Island or a dwarf lupine from Crater Lake. Faba means "bean" in Latin; members of this family bear large seeds in single-chambered pods. *Fabaceae* also have a showy upper petal to attract bees (called a "banner" or "standard"), as well as two wing petals for the bees to land on, and two petals joined together (a "keel") in the middle to protect their vitals.

Some plant families can be very large—there are over twenty thousand members of both the orchid and the aster families world-wide—and so botanists further divide the flowers within a family according to genus. Each genus has classic characteristics (think "generic"). Finally, individual flowers that are genetically identical enough to produce offspring are considered to be of the same species (as in "specific").

Becoming acquainted with the scientific names of a few favorite wildflowers can lead to a better appreciation of how they are related to one another and how they function. The common monkeyflower, *Mimulus guttatus*, is a good example of how scientific names can help us to understand a plant. This flower is in the family *scrophulariaceae*, whose members were once used to treat scrofula, a rather terrifying affliction of the lymph nodes. The genus name *Mimulus* comes from the Latin word for an actor that performs in mimes or farces, and was given to the monkey-flowers because of their grinning, masklike blooms. *Guttatus*, meaning "speckled," describes the little red dots on the common monkeyflower's throat, which serve to guide bees to its nectar.

Latin names can also sometimes connect us Euro-Americans to our own mythic past, a time when we lived much closer to nature. Take the case of yarrow, for example. Wherever yarrow is found, local people have learned to use it as a remedy. Pacific Northwest people are familiar with its healing potential: the Squaxin have used it as a stomach tonic, the Squamish to cure measles, the Tsimshian as a sore throat gargle, and the Cowichan as a blood purifier. The plant's generic name, *Achillea*, informs people from cultures originating in Europe (where the plant also grows) of its curative properties, for the legendary hero Achilles is said to have used it to treat the wounds of his soldiers at Troy.

DUTCHMAN'S BREECHES
Dicentra cucullaria

Horsetail Falls-Oneonta Loop Trail
Columbia River Gorge Scenic Area
Mount Hood National Forest
Cascade Range, Oregon
April 7, 1996

> *More than other plant groups, the flowering plants are ecologically related to animals. Modern animals, including humans, and flowering plants are equally dependent upon each other.*
>
> —FRANK B. SALISBURY

I have often wondered why flowering plants offer so many remedies for human ailments. Of course, we all know that the chemicals in plants perform certain functions that benefit the plants themselves (mostly by fending off the animals who would otherwise eat them), but it is amazing to me how many of these chemicals can also help to heal human injuries and illnesses. Wild plants also provide lots of useful materials. Native people of the Pacific Northwest have long gathered much of what they need for medicine, food, and clothing from flowering plants.

One afternoon last spring, I wandered through a garden with ethnobotanist Julie Cordero, a California Chumash woman who was raised in Seattle. As we encountered

OVAL-LEAFED BUCKWHEAT
Erigonum ovalifolium var. *nivale*
YARROW
Achillea millefolium var. *alpicola*
Head of Big Indian Gorge
Steens Mountain
Andrews Resource Area
Bureau of Land Management
Harney County, Oregon
August 5, 1997

each plant, she explained many of its medicinal and material uses, at one point even showing me a pretty braid of milkweed fiber fastened around her ankle. "I don't get it!" I blurted out, finally. "Why should all these plants be so useful to us?"

"Well," she began, "Our old stories teach us how to take only our share of plants—to thin them or cut them back just enough to help them flourish—and to give them something, maybe a pinch of tobacco, in return. Some plants that are really useful, I invite them to grow around my doorway. I like to weave baskets and so in the fall, I visit the juncus rushes and massage the mud around their roots with my feet. Those rushes grow better the next spring if I take care of them like that." A few days later, I took a walk on the beach with a university botanist and a high school biology teacher. When I told them what Julie had said, both suddenly stopped plodding along the sand, looked at each other in amazement, and exclaimed: "Those plants are using us!"

A geneticist might agree that certain aspects of what we consider to be wild plants may have evolved due to the attentions of humans over the centuries. We know, for example, that the Skagit and Snohomish managed their land by burning it to encourage the growth of useful plants and further enhanced their local food supply by propagating staples such as camas, brackenfern, and many different berries. This process can be explained in the scientific, cause-and-effect language of chromosomes and cultivation. But Julie went a little farther. To her way of thinking, both plants and people benefit from these exchanges not only in a practical sense, but in the satisfaction of having a good relationship with one another. She put it this way, "We have to really care for others if we want them to care for us."

And our sisters are the roots and berries. And you would treat them as such. Their life to you is just as important as another person would be.
—MARGARET SALUSKIN, YAKAMA

Traditional stories of the Pacific Northwest's indigenous cultures—the Yakama, the Hoh, the Duwamish, the Samish, the Nez Perce, and so many others—are often assumed by European-Americans to be naive attempts to explain things that pre-scientific people could not understand. In recent years, however, these stories have been revealed as a remarkably effective way to transmit knowledge about a world that, in fact, these cultures understood very intimately. What once seemed like charming but pointless tales actually contain a considerable amount of information, such as which plants to collect for what purpose, what to expect at what season, and how to treat the world and each other.

Long ago, according to a Skagit story, a canoe builder noticed that some salmon berries were ripening. He reached way up to pull off some of the reddest ones, but they pulled him off instead, right up off the earth and into the sky! Everyone—Black Bear and Elk, Beaver and Chickadee, and even Steelhead and Sucker—had to undertake a perilous journey to the sky to bring him back.

One moral of this tale is that a single person's actions can affect a whole community. Another lesson it holds is: never eat the first berries that look ripe. After all, although they may not snatch you away entirely, they can certainly make you ill. A third lesson dates back to the old days, when salmonberry patches belonged to certain people. There were serious consequences if anyone else took berries from a patch before its owner had harvested enough for a feast.

Perhaps most importantly, this story encourages its listeners to remember that the familiar plants that surround us every day are living beings. Rather than take them for granted, we should respect them. After all, our lives are inextricable from the lives of plants. What we do to them will have consequences for us as well.

NAKED BROOMRAPE
Orobanche uniflora var. *minuta*

MINER'S LETTUCE
Montia perfoliata

SMALL-FLOWERED BLUE-EYED-MARY
Collinsia parviflora

Indian Cliffs Trail
Heyburn State Park
Benewah County, Idaho
May 16, 1996

> *Shine! Shine! Shine!*
> *Pour down your warmth, great Sun!*
> *While we bask—we two together.*
> 　　—WALT WHITMAN, *Out of the Cradle Endlessly Rocking*

One recent summer afternoon, a friend and I strolled a woodland trail in the Three Sisters Wilderness that was dotted with star lilies, delphinium, and yarrow. Suddenly, we found ourselves surrounded by seepspring arnica and common monkeyflowers. Kneeling for a closer look, I soaked my knees in a rivulet of water concealed in the needles of the forest floor. Now that we knew it was there, we could easily see where the little stream wound off through the forest because of the waterloving monkeyflowers and arnica blossoming along its course. Simple observations like this have given rise to the notion that plants form "communities" such as the forest floor community, the streamside community, and so on.

However, repeated studies show that plants are opportunists that grow wherever they can and that there are no boundaries defining any such thing as a plant community. Yarrow, for instance, blooms almost everywhere from beach to meadow to mountaintop and may be found in mild habitats like Whidbey Island with western buttercups and broadleaf stonecrop, or in more extreme conditions like Oregon's Steens Mountain together with oval-leaved buckwheat and arrowleaf groundsel.

It seems that plants form communities the way that people do. When we find a place we like—whether we are born there or blown there by circumstances—we put down roots. As climate and other factors such as the course of a stream change over time, some plants drop out of communities while new ones join them. As William K. Stevens wrote in the New York Times: "Ecologists increasingly are abandoning the popular concept of the balance of nature and are replacing it with the image of a natural world in which plant and animal communities perpetually fluctuate."

With or without community boundaries, plants that live together contribute to each other's wellbeing in many ways. Large flowering plants such as Gray's lovage provide shade and support for smaller plants, cooling and shielding them from the scorching sun and drying wind and also serving as trellises for climbing flowers such as coast manroot. Ninety-five percent of land plants are thought to support fungi called *mycorrhizae* in their roots, with which they exchange substances with other plants and obtain minerals from the soil while providing their fungal partners with sugars (this is why it is usually futile to try and transplant flora from the wild, since garden soils lack the proper *mycorrhizae*). Some plants create better soil conditions for others by breaking up or dissolving rock, or by trapping dirt in which others may grow. Lupines and clovers enrich the soil by means of the nitrogen-fixing bacteria that inhabit their roots. Slender paintbrush are just the opposite, pilfering nourishment from the roots of other plants. And in the end, all plants aerate and add nutrients to the soil as they die and decompose into humus.

Flowers themselves are a good reason for certain plants to live together. Showy masses of flowers stand a better chance of attracting bird, bat, or insect pollinators than single ones do. Flowers may even resemble one another, as in the case of buttercups and cinquefoils, in order to increase everyone's chances of attracting flies or beetles or bees.

Wildflowers remind us that few plants lead solitary lives. Every flowering plant provides shelter or nourishment for a host of other plants, insects, birds, reptiles, and mammals. The relationships of flowering plants with each other and with all sorts of animals provide a model of how individuals may thrive within communities of many, diverse members. Flowers can reconcile us to other forms of life, no matter how unappealing. Entomologist Friedrich G. Barth points out that mosquitoes, for instance, are very important pollinators and that the males, at least, "are content to suck nectar." He adds: "our relationship to these hastily and unjustly condemned creatures could be considerably better."

BROADLEAF LUPINE
Lupinus latifolius
BRACTED LOUSEWORT
Pedicularis bracteosa var. *latifolia*
MAGENTA PAINTBRUSH
Castilleja parviflora var. *oreopola*
SUBALPINE DAISY
Erigeron peregrinus var. *callianthemus*

Skyline Trail, Paradise Park
Mount Rainier National Park
Cascade Range, Washington
August 5, 1996

> *The sea is where we came from.*
> *Rivers are how we got here.*
> —DAVID QUAMMEN, *Natural Acts*

Some friends and I once spent an evening talking about where we grew up. There were eight of us, each from a different part of the country, and yet every one of us remembered a nearby stream where we had gone as children, just to watch the life in and surrounding the water. The Pacific Northwest is laced with such streams. Rainfall and snowmelt sustain year-round rivers from the coastal ranges to the sea;

tendrils of water wind down from the interior mountains and wander across dry interior valleys, forming a dendritic (tree-like) pattern that connects the interior of the Pacific Northwest to the ocean just as our blood vessels bind our bodies to our hearts.

    The Snake and the Salmon rivers begin at the Continental Divide in the mountains of Idaho and their waters make their way clear to the Pacific, part of the Columbia River system whose tributaries at one time carried life—plant, animal, and human—both to and from the ocean. Now a source of hydroelectric power for lighting and machines, the Columbia has a much longer history as the circulatory system of the Pacific Northwest, the unifying force of a living bioregion. Rivers are corridors of migration, regardless of the direction of their flow. Seeds and bits of plants drift downstream, but they may also travel upstream. Rooting along sources of moisture wherever they can reach and survive, plants extend their range in alternately widening and contracting colonies.

> *Believe me when I say…*
> *water is the skin of the earth.*
> —LUIS RODRIGUEZ, *Believe Me When I Say*

    Most of the moisture that falls in the Pacific Northwest comes in the winter and spring, but flowering plants help some of it to remain in place throughout the year. A canopy of living plants shades moist soil. Leaves are made up largely of water—any cookbook will tell you to use only a third as much of a dried herb as a fresh one. Plants retain water in their leaves with an array of strategies from oils and resins to thick skins and tiny hairs. Intertwining root systems also act like a sponge to bond the soil with moisture, and layers of fallen leaves and petals protect the ground from erosive runoff and from the drying sun and wind.

    However, this sheltering cloak of vegetation does not remain static over time. In the forest, ancient trees eventually die and keel over, creating holes in the canopy. Fires burn gaps in the ground covers of prairies as well as woodlands. These openings are recolonized by various plants that flourish when exposed to sunlight and mineral soil, resulting in a healthy "mosaic" of diverse plant communities. Nature heals its vegetative wounds by a process known as plant succession, in which early colonizers are eventually overwhelmed by the very plants they have sheltered and provided for. We know that the natural world can heal itself and see it coping just fine with destruction on a certain scale, but we really don't know how much it can take.

Land managers from Forest Service biologists to city planners endeavor to assess how far we can go in destroying the plants and soils of our own habitat, but the consequences are pretty difficult to predict. When we read a newspaper account of legal efforts to block development in order to save a few posies we have never heard of, sometimes we don't know whether we should laugh or cry. Are people foolish to worry about the welfare of plants versus the potential benefits of more dams, more highways, more housing materials, and more jobs?

In 1997, abundant rains sluiced soils downslope all over western Oregon and Washington. Unchecked by trees or understory plants, landslides tore gaping holes in hillsides, carried off people's homes and possessions, and buried roads. Few denied that clear-cutting the forested slopes had been a bad idea, but efforts to protect the forest ecosystem for its own sake had not been taken seriously. Sometimes there is no way to prevent such disasters except by invoking the name of an obscure flower, which often has a silly-sounding name—one memorable plaintiff is known as tall bugbane—in a court of law.

UPLAND LARKSPUR
Delphinium nuttallianum var. *nuttallianum*

COLUMBIA DESERT PARSLEY
Lomatium columbianum

Mayer State Park
Highway 30
Columbia River Gorge
Wasco County, Oregon
April 22, 1997

When an affection for a particular plant or tree is aroused in us we are linked through an emotional bond, more subtle and immediate than the effect of scent, to the greater world of vegetation of which the plant or tree is a part. It is a deep, wise world…
—WILLIAM ANDERSON, *The Green Man*

COLUMBIA LEWISIA
Lewisia columbiana var. *columbiana*
Slate Peak, Forest Road 5400
Mount Baker-Snoqualamie
National Forest
North Cascade Range, Washington
August 3, 1997

When most of us think of the Pacific Northwest, usually its forests come to mind. The region is home not only to the temperate rainforest but also to Douglas fir forests on the lower slopes of drier mountains and the subalpine forests of higher elevations. All of these forests are more than just trees—they are mosses, lichens, ferns, and fungi, shrubs and wildflowers, forming canopies and carpets and masses of green. In a sense, forests are the heart of the plant world, places where we humans cannot help but connect to the realm where chlorophyll is king.

Old-growth forests are often compared to cathedrals, and architectural historians trace a connection between the Gothic cathedrals of the Old World and the groves of trees where Europeans once worshipped. When the light is just right and the flower-sprinkled avenues between trees recede invitingly into the shadows, sometimes it seems as though we are not alone in the woods any more, not separated from nature after all.

Our European ancestors imbued forests with the presence of the Green Man, a figure whose face and limbs are composed of leaves. Gothic artisans often depicted Green Men in churches, carved atop pillars or gazing from ceilings. Scholar William Anderson finds a link between artistic revivals of the Green Man (who is sometimes a Green Woman) and periods when artists sense that the human bond with nature is threatened—as, for instance, during the rise of industrialization in Britain. According to Kootenai tribal member Gayle Highpine, native people of the Pacific Northwest believe that Sasquatch—Bigfoot is also most often seen at times when the relationship between people and the earth is troubled. Lurking in the woods and munching on rhododendrons, Sasquatch keeps a watchful eye on how we treat the other forms of life with whom we share this green and growing world.

 *Susan Lamb*

STREAM VIOLET *Viola glabella*

Lower Trail, The Nature Conservancy's Cascade Head Preserve
Tillamook County, Oregon
April 3, 1996

Mission bells
Fritillaria lanceolata

Sitka Valerian
Valeriana sitchensis

Forest Road 2610
Dosewallips River Canyon
Olympic National Forest
Olympic Mountains, Washington
April 5, 1996

COLUMBIA KITTENTAILS
Synthyris stellata

Horsetail Falls-Oneonta Loop Trail
Columbia River Gorge National Scenic Area
Mount Hood National Forest
Cascade Range, Oregon
April 7, 1996

LARGE-FLOWERED BLUE-EYED MARY
Collinsia grandiflora

ROSY PLECTRITIS
Plectritis congesta

Lower Table Rock Trail
The Nature Conservancy's
Lower Table Rock Preserve
Jackson County, Oregon
April 9, 1996

Showy phlox
Phlox speciosa

Arrowleaf balsamroot
Balsamorhiza sagittata

Hills above Columbia River
Highway 28 near Trinidad
Douglas County, Washington
April 23, 1997

PUSSY EARS *Calochortus tolmiei*

Lower Table Rock Trail
The Nature Conservancy's Lower Table Rock Preserve
Jackson County, Oregon
April 9, 1996

FAIRY LANTERN
Disporum smithii

FALSE LILY-OF-THE-VALLEY
Maianthemum dilatatum

Sunset Bay State Park
Coos County, Oregon
April 12, 1987

SKUNK CABBAGE *Lysichitum americanum*

Cape Blanco with Gull and Castle Rocks
Cape Blanco State Park, Curry County, Oregon
April 12, 1987

FEW FLOWERED SHOOTING STAR *Dodecatheon pulchellum* var. *pulchellum*

Riverside State Park
Spokane County, Washington
April 28, 1996

Arrowleaf balsamroot
Balsamorhiza sagittata

Columbia desert parsley
Lomatium columbianum

Mayer State Park
Highway 30, Columbia River Gorge
Wasco County, Oregon
April 22, 1997

BEACH PEA *Lathyrus japonicus*

San Juan Island Historical Park
San Juan Island, San Juan County, Washington
April 24, 1997

FAIRY SLIPPER
Calypso bulbosa
~ and Douglas fir cones
Lime Kiln Point State Park
San Juan Island
San Juan County, Washington
April 24, 1997

COMMON CAMAS
Camassia quamash var. *maxima*
MANROOT
Marah oreganus
Turtleback Mountain
Deer Harbor Road, Orcas Island
San Juan County, Washington
April 24, 1997

RED BESSEYA
Besseya rubra

Ina H. Johnston Natural Area
Dishman Hills Natural Resource
Conservation Area
Spokane County, Washington
April 27, 1996

GIANT FAWN LILY *Erythronium oregonum*

Westside Road, San Juan Island
San Juan County, Washington
April 24, 1997

DEL NORTE COUNTY IRIS *Iris innominata*

Rouge River Canyon near Galice
Galice Resource Area, Bureau of Land Management
Josephine County, Oregon
April 26, 1997

Purple trillium
Trillium petiolatum

Western spring beauty
Claytonia lanceolata var. *lanceolata*

Stream Violet
Viola glabella

Tumwater Canyon
Wenatchee National Forest
Cascade Range, Washington
April 29, 1996

SCOULER'S CORYDALIS
Corydalis scouleri

Queets River Road
Queets River Rainforest
Olympic National Park
Olympic Mountains, Washington
May 2, 1996

COMMON CAMAS
Camassia quamash var. *maxima*
YARROW
Achillea millefolium var. *californica*
WESTERN BUTTERCUP
Ranunculus occidentalis

Deception Pass
Deception Pass State Park
Whidbey Island
Island County, Washington
May 1, 1996

OREGON ANEMONE
Anemone oregana var. *oregana*

WESTERN SPRING BEAUTY
Claytonia lanceolata var. *lanceolata*

STREAM VIOLET
Viola glabella

Tumwater Canyon
Wenatchee National Forest
Cascade Range, Washington
April 29, 1996

BROADLEAF STONECROP
Sedum spathulifolium
Deception Pass
Deception Pass State Park
Whidbey Island
Island County, Washington
May 1, 1996

Seashore lupine
Lupinus littoralis
Umpqua Dunes
Oregon Dunes National Recreation Area
Siuslaw National Forest, Oregon
April 31, 1981

PACIFIC RHODODENDRON
Rhododendron macrophyllum

Oregon Dunes National Recreation Area
Siuslaw National Forest, Oregon
May 2, 1981

COAST FAWN LILY
Erythronium revolutum

Saddle Mountain State Park
Coast Range
Clatsop County, Oregon
May 3, 1996

PACIFIC BLEEDINGHEART
Dicentra formosa
— and lady ferns

Silver Falls Loop Trail
Silver Falls State Park
Cascade Range
Marion County, Oregon
May 13, 1997

SEASHORE LUPINE *Lupinus littoralis*
FIELD CHICKWEED *Cerastium arvense*

Cape Perpetua Viewpoint, Siuslaw National Forest
Lincoln County, Oregon
May 3, 1996

OWYHEE CLOVER
Trifolium owyheense

Leslie Gulch
Malheur Resource Area
Bureau of Land Management
Malheur County, Oregon
May 12, 1996

UPLAND LARKSPUR
Delphinium nuttallianum var. *muttallianum*
Klamath Falls-Lakeview Highway
Whiskey Creek Valley
Winema National Forest, Oregon
May 11, 1996

WHITE-RAYED WYETHIA *Wyethia helianthoides*

Highway 55, Little Goose Creek Valley
Payette National Forest, Idaho
May 16, 1997

PALE EVENING-PRIMROSE
Oenothera pallida

Sand dunes near Wanapum Lake
Junction of Highways 26 and 243
Grant County, Washington
May 14, 1997

ARROWLEAF BALSAMROOT
Balsamorhiza sagittata
Leslie Gulch
Leslie Gulch Wilderness Study Area
Malheur Resource Area
Bureau of Land Management
Malheur County, Oregon
May 12, 1996

PURPLE SAGE *Salvia dorrii* var. *carnosa*
LINEAR-LEAF DAISY *Erigeron linearis*

Highway 243 near Wanapum Lake, Bureau of Reclamation Lands
Grant County, Washington
May 17, 1996

NAKED BROOMRAPE *Orobanche uniflora* var. *minuta*
MINER'S LETTUCE *Montia perfoliata*

Indian Cliffs Trail, Heyburn State Park
Benewah County, Idaho
May 16, 1996

VASEFLOWER *Clematis hirsutissima*

West Side Road, Meadows Valley
New Meadows, Adams County, Idaho
May 15, 1997

LARGE-FLOWERED TONELLA
Tonella floribunda
Highway 12
Snake River Canyon
near Clarkston, Washington
May 14, 1997

WHITE-STEMMED SWERTIA
Swertia albicaulis

Northrup Canyon
Castle Rock Natural Area Preserve
Steamboat Rock State Park
Grant County, Washington
May 17, 1996

Heart-leaf arnica
Arnica cordifolia var. *cordifolia*
Starry solomon's seal
Smilacina stellata
Indian Cliffs Trail
Heyburn State Park
Benewah County, Idaho
May 16, 1996

LITTLE LARKSPUR
Delphinium bicolor

NINE-LEAF LOMATIUM
Lomatium triternatum

PINK MICROSTERIS
Microsteris gracilis

White Bird Battlefield Auto Tour
Salmon River Canyon
Idaho County, Idaho
May 15, 1997

THREADLEAF PHACELIA
Phacelia linearis
APPLEGATE'S PAINTBRUSH
Castilleja applegatei
Highway 95 near Lucile
Salmon River Canyon
Idaho County, Idaho
May 15, 1997

Columbia milk-vetch
Astragalus succumbens

Highway 243 near Wanapum Lake
Bureau of Reclamation Lands
Grant County, Washington
May 17, 1996

WESTERN RHODODENDRON
Rhododendron macrophyllum
~ State Flower of Washington

Mount Walker Road
Olympic National Forest
Jefferson County, Washington
May 29, 1997

BALDHIP ROSE *Rosa gymnocarpa*

South Whidbey State Park, Whidbey Island
Island County, Washington
May 30, 1997

WESTERN TWINFLOWER
Linnaea borealis
South Whidbey State Park
Whidbey Island
Island County, Washington
May 30, 1997

WOODNYMPH
Pyrola uniflora

Spruce Trail
Hoh River Rainforest
Olympic National Park
Olympic Peninsula, Washington
May 28, 1997

FRAGRANT POPCORN FLOWER
Plagiobothrys figuratus

The Nature Conservancy's Tom McCall Preserve
Highway 30, Columbia River Gorge
Wasco County, Oregon
May 27, 1997

SHRUBBY PENSTEMON
Penstemon fruticosus var. *fruticosus*
Highway 2, Tumwater Canyon
Wenatchee National Forest
Cascade Range, Washington
May 30, 1997

HOOKER ONION *Allium acuminatum*

Highway 2 near Highland
Douglas County, Washington
May 30, 1997

COLUMBIA CLEMATIS
Clematis columbiana
Mineral Ridge Trail
Highway 97, Coeur d'Alene Scenic Byway
Kootenai County, Idaho
May 31, 1997

HYACINTH BRODIAEA
Brodiaea hyacinthina
The Nature Conservancy's Tom McCall Preserve
Highway 30, Columbia River Gorge
Wasco County, Oregon
May 27, 1997

TWEEDY'S LEWISIA
Lewisia tweedyi

Highway 2, Tumwater Canyon
Wenatchee National Forest
Cascade Range, Washington
May 30, 1996

DOUGLAS IRIS *Iris douglasii*

Devil's Backbone, Siskiyou National Forest
Siskiyou Mountains, Curry County, Oregon
May 20, 1987

DOUGLAS IRIS
Iris douglasii

The Heads above Nellie Cove
Port Orford Heads State Park
Curry County, Oregon
May 22, 1987

BIGLEAF LUPINE *Lupinus polyphyllus* var. *burkei*
MEADOW BUTTERCUP *Ranunculus acris* [European alien]

Gotham Bay, Highway 97, Coeur d'Alene Scenic Byway
Kootenai County, Idaho
May 31, 1997

NORTHERN WYETHIA
Wyethia amplexicaulis

Highway 129 near Rattlesnake Summit
Asotin County, Washington
June 1, 1997

Spotted coral-root
Corallorhiza maculata
Indian Cliffs Trail
Heyburn State Park
Benewah County, Idaho
June 1, 1997

GIANT HELLEBORINE *Epipactis gigantea*

The Nature Conservancy's Thousand Springs Preserve, Snake River Plain
Gooding County, Idaho
June 3, 1996

BIG-HEAD CLOVER
Trifolium macrocephalum

Highway 3
Wallowa County, Oregon
June 1, 1997

ELKHORNS CLARKIA
Clarkia pulchella

Ukiah Hillgard Highway
Grande Ronde River Canyon
near Red Bridge State Park
Union County, Oregon
June 2, 1997

Dwarf monkeyflower
Mimulus nanus

Loop Road
Craters of the Moon National Monument
Butte County, Idaho
June 4, 1996

GLAND CINQUEFOIL
Potentilla glandulosa

ANTELOPE BITTERBRUSH
Purshia tridentata

Lava Cascades
Craters of the Moon National Monument
Butte County, Idaho
June 4, 1996

CUSICK'S SUNFLOWER *Helianthus cusickii*

Painted Hills Unit, John Day Fossil Beds National Monument
Wheeler County, Oregon
June 2, 1997

GOLDEN SPIDERFLOWER *Cleome platycarpa*

Painted Hills Unit, John Day Fossil Beds National Monument
Wheeler County, Oregon
June 2, 1997

HARSH PAINTBRUSH
Castilleja hispida var. *hispida*
SPREADING PHLOX
Phlox diffusa

Saddle Mountain State Park
Coast Range
Clatsop County, Oregon
June 7, 1996

Yellow monkeyflower
Mimulus guttatus var. *depauperatus*

Rosy plectritis
Plectritis congesta

Saddle Mountain State Park
Coast Range
Clatsop County, Oregon
June 7, 1996

ORANGE HONEYSUCKLE
Lonicera ciliosa
~ and Ponderosa pine
Metolius River Trail
Deschutes National Forest
Cascade Range, Oregon
June 29, 1996

CLIFF PENSTEMON
Penstemon rupicola
Highway 706 near Narada Falls
Mount Rainier National Park
Cascade Range, Washington
June 27, 1997

BUNCHBERRY *Cornus canadensis*
~ with mosses and lichens

Roaring River Trail, Willamette National Forest
Cascade Range, Oregon
June 28, 1996

OREGON SEDUM
Sedum oreganum

Buckeye Lake
Rogue-Umpqua Divide Wilderness
Umpqua National Forest, Cascade Range
Douglas County, Oregon
June 18, 1986

ELEPHANT'S HEAD
Pedicularis groenlandica
SLENDER PAINTBRUSH
Castilleja gracillima
Duck Lake
Payette Crest
Payette National Forest, Idaho
June 19, 1987

BEARGRASS *Xerophyllum tenax* – with aspens

Lick Creek Road, Payette Crest
Payette National Forest, Idaho
June 19, 1987

SUKSDORF'S PAINTBRUSH
Castilleja suksdorfii

Mt. Jefferson from Jefferson Park
Jefferson Peak Wilderness
Willamette National Forest
Cascade Range, Oregon
July 9, 1985

ALPINE LAUREL
Kalmia microphylla
~ and Bachelor Butte

Sparks Lake
Cascades Loop Highway
Deschutes National Forest
Cascade Range, Oregon
June 30, 1996

AVALANCHE LILY
Erythronium montanum
Bench Lake Trail
Mount Rainier National Park
Cascade Range, Washington
June 27, 1997

Syringa
Philadelphus lewisii
~ State Flower of Idaho

Lapwai Creek Canyon
Highway 95
Lewis County, Idaho
June 28, 1997

Western white trillium
Trillium ovatum

Avalanche lily
Erythronium montanum

Bench Lake Trail
Mt. Rainier National Park
Cascade Range, Washington
June 27, 1997

WHITE BOG-ORCHID
Habenaria dilatata

BIGLEAF LUPINE
Lupinus polyphyllus var. *burkei*

Metolius River Trail
Deschutes National Forest
Cascade Range, Oregon
June 28, 1996

Skunk-leaved polemonium
Polemonium pulcherrimum
False hellebore
Veratrum californicum
Hood River Meadows
Mt. Hood National Forest
Cascade Range, Oregon
June 30, 1996

BUNCHBERRY
Cornus canadensis

WESTERN WHITE ANEMONE
Anemone deltoidea

Roaring River Trail
Willamette National Forest
Cascade Range, Oregon
June 28, 1996

Cow parsnip *Heracleum lanatum*
Red columbine *Aquilegia formosa*
Broadleaf lupine *Lupinus latifolius*
Arrowleaf groundsel *Groundsel triangularis*

Linton Springs, Linton Meadows
Three Sisters Wilderness, Willamette National Forest
Cascade Range, Lane County, Oregon
July 23, 1987

STREAMBANK ARNICA *Arnica amplexicaulis*

Tamanawas Falls, Mount Hood Wilderness
Mount Hood National Forest
Cascade Range, Oregon
July 14, 1985

SCARLET PAINTBRUSH
Castilleja miniata

WESTERN PASQUEFLOWER
Anemone occidentalis

Timberline Trail, Elk Cove
Mt. Hood Wilderness
Mt. Hood National Forest
Cascade Range, Oregon
July 13, 1985

SUKSDORF'S PAINTBRUSH
Castilleja suksdorfii

COLUMBIA LARKSPUR
Delphinium trolliifolium

Canyon Creek Meadows
Mount Jefferson Wilderness
Deschutes National Forest
Cascade Range, Oregon
July 11, 1985

BACH'S DOWNINGIA
Downingia bacigalupii

Vernal pools along Silver Creek
Sage Hen Valley
Highway 20, near Riley
Harney County, Oregon
June 30, 1997

DAVIDSON'S PENSTEMON
Penstemon davidsonii
McKenzie Pass
Willamette National Forest
Cascade Range, Oregon
July 4, 1986

RED MOUNTAIN-HEATHER
Phyllodoce empetriformis

Pacific Crest Trail
Naches Peak
Wenatchee National Forest
Cascade Range, Washington
August 4, 1996

BROADLEAF LUPINE
Lupinus latifolius

AMERICAN BISTORT
Polygonum bistortoides

Hurricane Ridge near Eagle Point
Olympic National Park
Olympic Mountains, Washington
August 1, 1997

Tiger lily
Lilium columbianum

Cow parsnip
Heracleum lanatum

Mt. Angeles Road
Hurricane Ridge
Olympic National Park
Olympic Mountains, Washington
August 1, 1997

MERTEN'S MOUNTAIN HEATHER
Cassiope mertensiana var. *mertensiana*

Heather Meadows
Mt. Baker-Snoqualamie National Forest
North Cascade Range, Washington
August 2, 1996

GLACIER LILY *Erythronium grandiflorum* var. *grandiflorum*

Skyline Trail, Paradise Park
Mount Rainier National Park, Cascade Range, Washington
August 1, 1997

GLACIER LILY
Erythronium grandiflorum var. *grandiflorum*

WESTERN PASQUEFLOWER
Anemone occidentalis
~ and the Tatoosh Range

Skyline Trail, Paradise Park
Mount Rainier National Park
Cascade Range, Washington
July 31, 1997

PINEDROPS
Pterospora andromedea
Ohanapecosh River Trail
Mount Rainier National Park
Cascade Range, Washington
August 4, 1996

NODDING ONION
Allium cernuum
SCARLET PAINTBRUSH
Castilleja miniata var. *miniata*
Blue Mountain near Deer Park
Olympic National Park
Olympic Mountains, Washington
August 1, 1996

BROADLEAF LUPINE *Lupinus latifolius*
SITKA VALERIAN *Valeriana sitchensis*
WESTERN PASQUEFLOWER *Anemone occidentalis*

Mount Rainier from the Skyline Trail, Paradise Park
Mount Rainier National Park, Cascade Range, Washington
August 6, 1996

MOUNTAIN BOG GENTIAN
Gentiana calycosa var. *calycosa*
Lakes Trail near Reflection Lakes
Mount Rainier National Park
Cascade Range, Washington
August 6, 1996

LEAFY ARNICA
Arnica chamissonis var. *incana*
Sparks Lake and South Sister
Deschutes National Forest
Cascade Range, Oregon
August 3, 1988

ORANGE SNEEZEWEED *Helenium hoopesii*
FIVE-FINGERED CINQUEFOIL *Potentilla gracilis*

Big Indian Gorge, Steens Mountain
Andrews Resource Area, Bureau of Land Management
Harney County, Oregon
August 5, 1997

ELKSLIP MARSHMARIGOLD *Caltha leptosepala* var. *leptosepala*

Headwaters Little Blitzen River, Steens Mountain
Andrews Resource Area, Bureau of Land Management
Harney County, Oregon
August 4, 1997

TWINFLOWER MARSHMARIGOLD
Caltha biflora var. *biflora*

Golden Gate Trail, Paradise Park
Mount Rainier National Park
Cascade Range, Washington
August 4, 1996

TAPER-LEAVED PENSTEMON *Penstemon attenuatus* var. *militaris*
SILKY LUPINE *Lupinus sericeus* var. *sericeus* SCARLET PAINTBRUSH *Castilleja miniata* var. *miniata*
FALSE HELLEBORE *Veratrum californicum* var. *californicum* ALPINE KNOTWEED *Polygonum phytolaccaefolium*

Trinity Mountain
Boise National Forest, Idaho
August 6, 1997

WIDE-FRUIT MARIPOSA *Calochortus eurycarpus*
TAPER-LEAVED PENSTEMON *Penstemon attenuatus* var. *militaris*

Near Big Trinity Lake, Trinity Mountain
Boise National Forest, Idaho
August 6, 1997

LEWIS MONKEYFLOWER
Mimulus lewisii

Kerr Valley
Crater Lake National Park
Cascade Range, Oregon
August 12, 1996

ELEPHANT'S-HEAD
Pedicularis groenlandica
SUBALPINE BUTTERCUP
Ranunculus eschscholtzii
LARGE MOUNTAIN MONKEYFLOWER
Mimulus tilingii
Eagle Cap
Eagle Cap Wilderness
Wallowa-Whitman National Forest
Wallowa Mountains, Oregon
August 8, 1985

Lewis monkeyflower
Mimulus lewisii
Seep spring arnica
Arnica longifolia
Kerr Valley
Crater Lake National Park
Cascade Range, Oregon
August 12, 1996

FIREWEED
Epilobium angustifolium

SEEP SPRING ARNICA
Arnica longifolia

Vidae Falls, Rim Drive
Crater Lake National Park
Cascade Range, Oregon
August 12, 1996

WIDE-FRUIT MARIPOSA
Calochortus eurycarpus

PALISH INDIAN PAINTBRUSH
Castilleja pallescens

Near Big Trinity Lake
Trinity Mountain
Boise National Forest, Idaho
August 7, 1997

Photographer's Notes

I used an assortment of photographic equipment in making these images. My primary tools since 1975 have been several generations of Arca-Swiss view cameras which I shoot in both 4x5 and 2¼ and 2¾ formats. The 4x5 works best for the grand landscapes, the 2¼ and 2¾ for close-ups. Most 35mm work was done with a Nikkor 60mm f 2.8 micro lens on a Nikon 8008. I often used a polarizing screen for the view camera shots to reduce glare and contrast. For much of the close-up work I used flexible loops stretched with fabric, called Flex Fills, both to shield my subject from the wind and create soft light by shading. I also modified a Bogen tripod to lay flat on the ground. The images in this book were shot with Fuji Velvia and Kodak Ektachrome E100S film.